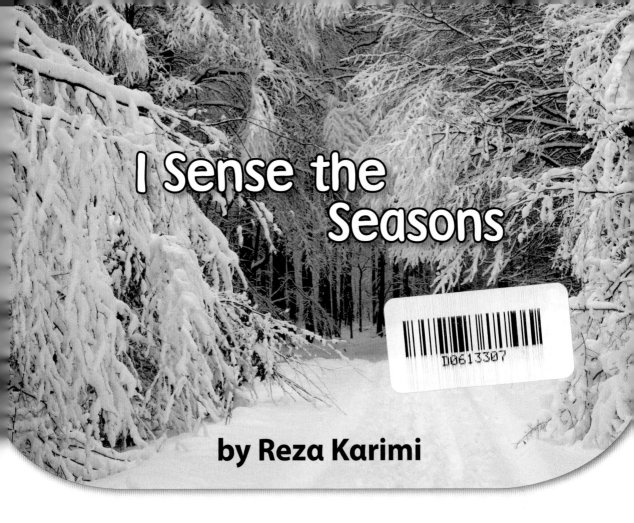

I Sense the Seasons

by Reza Karimi

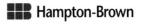

NATIONAL GEOGRAPHIC

Hampton-Brown

National Geographic and the Yellow Border are registered trademarks of the National Geographic Society.

National Geographic School Publishing
Hampton-Brown
www.NGSP.com

Printed in the USA.
Quad Graphics, Leominster, MA.

ISBN: 978-0-7362-7992-5

18 19   10 9

Acknowledgments and credits continue on the inside back cover.

I hear the wind.

I like fall. Do you like fall, too?

I see the snow.

I like winter. Do you like winter, too?

I smell the rain.

I like spring. Do you like spring, too?

**The sun is shining! I like summer.
Do you like summer, too?**